PARENTING FOR TEENS

- Diary Entry
- View Points
- Parental Tips
- Counsellor's Advice

Author
Seema Gupta

Published by:

F-2/16, Ansari Road, Daryaganj, New Delhi-110002
☎ 011-23240026, 011-23240027 • *Fax:* 011-23240028
Email: info@vspublishers.com • *Website:* www.vspublishers.com

Regional Office : Hyderabad
5-1-707/1, Brij Bhawan (Beside Central Bank of India Lane)
Bank Street, Koti, Hyderabad - 500 095
☎ 040-24737290
E-mail: vspublishershyd@gmail.com

Branch Office : Mumbai
Jaywant Industrial Estate, 2nd Floor–222, Tardeo Road
Opposite Sobo Central Mall, Mumbai – 400 034
☎ 022-23510736
E-mail vspublishersmum@gmail.com

Follow us on:

All books available at **www.vspublishers.com**

© Copyright: *V&S* PUBLISHERS
Edition 2017

The Copyright of this book, as well as all matter contained herein (including illustrations) rests with the Publisher. No person shall copy the name of the book, its title design, matter and illustrations in any form and in any language, totally or partially or in any form. Anybody doing so shall face legal action and will be responsible for damages.

Printed at Repro Knowledgecast Limited, Thane

Publisher's Note

V&S Publishers believes in bring forth books that are timely and in tune with current trends that cover the interests of wider sections of the society. This book is a reflection of parent-teen relationship. Good, bad or ugly- whichever way one likes to observe.

The teen years are a time of rapid growth, exploration, and risk taking. Taking risks provides young people the opportunity to test their skills and abilities and discover who they are. But, some risks—such as smoking, using drugs, drinking and driving, and having unprotected sex—can have harmful and long-lasting effects on a teen's health and well-being.

Parents are a powerful influence in the lives of their teens. When parents make a habit of knowing about their teens—what they are doing, who they are with, and where they are and setting clear expectations for behaviour with regular check-ins to be sure these expectations are being met—they can reduce their teens' risks for injury, pregnancy, and drug, alcohol, and cigarette use. These parents are monitoring their teens' activities and behavior.

Preface

The adolescents and young adults form that salient section of our vast and diverse society which is perplexed about their own position, for their age group is neither too big to be called a fully matured individual, nor too small to be called as children. Parents may try to help, but for some inexplicable reason, the adolescents tend to automatically close their two sense organs – the eyes and ears – to what their parents want them to see and hear.

Generally, the mindset of the adolescents is that parents are not their well-wishers. They are old-fashioned, rigid and dominating. This may be true sometimes and in certain cases, but not always. The youngsters feel that parents are good till they 'give in' and the moment they don't, they are *numero uno* enemy, which, they are certainly not.

However, the levels of stress that the adolescents face these days, at times does go beyond the comprehension of an adult mind. With modern electronic gadgets chipping in almost every other day, the lifestyle of the youngsters have completely transformed from what it was when their parents were teenagers. For example, an account on Facebook, today is considered to be a must to fit in their circle of friends. Calling each other is passe, the youngsters either chat on these sites or sms through their mobiles.

This may be difficult for the parents to comprehend as there is a big generation gap which needs to be bridged by sheer patience, faith and understanding on the part of both the parties.

In this book are given some *Diary Entry* from the diary of some adolescents who are marred with the problem, and try to resolve it in their own inimitable ways. Each diary entry is assessed and followed by a *Counsellor's Advice* which provides an amicable solution to the concerned problem in an unbiased manner.

In addition to all these, there is an exclusive *ParentalTip* at the end of each diary entry given by the author based on her own real life experiences, thoughts, realisations and a deep study of this ever rising conflict between parents or elders and the teenagers.

Contents

Conflict 1: Late Night Parties 9
Conflict 2: FB Fiasco 13
Conflict 3: Hole in My Pocket 17
Conflict 4: At Your Desk 21
Conflict 5: Remote Control 25
Conflict 6: Set Me Free 29
Conflict 7: What Do I Care! 33
Conflict 8: Attitude Problem 37
Conflict 9: Dating Blues 41
Conflict 10: Gymming 45
Conflict 11: Mobile Mania 49
Conflict 12: Tag Along 53
Conflict 13: My Friends…Your Friends 57
Conflict 14: Dressing Spells Doom 61
Conflict 15: Career Kit 65
Conflict 16: Playing Favourites 69
Conflict 17: The Locked Gate 73
Conflict 18: Boiling Over 77
Conflict 19: Nag… Nag… Nag… 81
Conflict 20: Food Row 85
Conflict 21: Exam Stress 89
Conflict 22: It's So Crowded 93
Conflict 23: I am Not Yours 97
Conflict 24: Special Needs 101
Conflict 25: Listen to Me 105
Adolesecnce *109*
Grievances *111*
Parenting Quiz *113*

Late Night Parties

Late night parties for teenagers are not acceptable in most Indian households, especially if the teenager is a girl. Does this mean the parents are too orthodox or is there any reasonable explanation to this rule that teenagers find so appalling?

Let's visit Malhotra household and see what Anushka and her parents say in this matter.

> **The middle class Malhotra household has following members:**
>
> Anushka — 16-years old teenager (student of class X)
> Rajesh — Anushka's father (employed in a marketing job)
> Suruchi — Anushka's mother (housewife)
> Abhinav — Anushka's brother (12-year old, student of class VII)

THE CONFLICT!!!

Anushka's Diary

Monday, September 26, after school

It was a fine day today. We had so much fun in school. The best part of my day was when this new girl Jenny invited me for her birthday party on Friday. She will be sixteen on September 30, so she is throwing a big party for all her friends at her place. Of course, her parents would be there too, but they are so cool. They do not interfere and let the kids have fun. And I have heard that the food her mom serves is always ordered from such fancy takeaway joints. Naturally, with all the money they can easily afford all that. Like always, this party will also go beyond my curfew time of 8pm so I wonder if my parents would give me permission to go. I did ask mom but she passed the buck to dad who is out of town and will only be back tomorrow evening.

Oooh! I have always wanted to go to her parties. All the others rave about them. Every time she invites me, mom throws a tantrum – Anu, there will be boys at the party. Dad has his own problems – Come back home by 8 latest. Come on now, whoever heard of ending a party at 8. Gosh, that's the time, the party begins. My other friends tell me that Jenny's parties go on till midnight. Cool man! That's the way it should be. Not like those dull and drab birthday parties that we have at home. First of all, mom insists on inviting only the girls for the party, besides some boys who are my friends since childhood. But they are like I know them from in and out. What is the fun in hanging out with them? Then some boring relatives and her kitty party friends also arrive. I agree they bring lots of gifts, but mingling with older crowd is just not so happening. Secondly, the party would begin at 5 or 6 in the evening for us kids. Although there is always good food that my mom cooks with lots of love and care and everyone praises her for that. She also arranges for some party games for all of us. But come now, we are teenagers not some piggy-tailed toddlers. Why can't they leave us alone once in a while? Then they would wind up the party by 8 or 8.30 for my friends but the older group stays till 10 or 11 with no one to show them the clock. My father also makes sure that all my friends reach home on time. I don't know why he is so stickler for rules. None of my friends complain though, in fact, they rather praise my father for this, but I know they would always prefer Jenny-type party than mine.

Oh, this is so infuriating. And coming back to my immediate problem, I am pretty sure that I will not be allowed to go for Jenny's party. I wonder if my little brother Abhinav will also have similar restrictions or are they just for me. I wish I had liberal parents who gave me enough space to live my own life.

I really wish...

Come to think of it I feel these are the problems which I need to discuss with my parents.

1. Why am I not allowed to go to late night parties when all the other girls can go?
2. Why should my father insist on my returning home by 8 pm?
3. What is the problem in partying with boys when we study together in a co-educational school?
4. Why are my own parties so boring and restricted?
5. Why does dad make sure that he drops all my friends to their homes personally?
6. Will my little brother Abhinav who is twelve years old now, be given the similar deadline when he grows up?
7. When will I be allowed to be on my own and live my life?

I wish they read my mind and give me answers to all the above questions which have been haunting me.

Anushka

Diary of Anushka's Mother
Counsellor Speaks

The problem between Anushka and her parents regarding late night parties stems from the root that many other girls are allowed to go to such parties, while Anushka's parents forbid her.

For Parents

- Parents should have a heart-to-heart talk with Anushka and clear her doubts. She should not feel as if she has been denied something because this may result in her turning into a rebel of sorts.
- The mother should also talk to Anushka and inform her about the vicious ways of life. Ramola and other people's experiences should be shared with her.
- Anushka's parents should also convey to her why they stick to their 8 pm deadline even for other girls who come to her parties. Give her some examples and make her realise the importance of this rule. If possible get your views endorsed by some of her friends. Once she understands she will not sulk over such a petty matter.
- Last but not the least, it may be advisable to let her hair down by allowing her to attend a late night party once in a while, but on condition that it should not cross beyond 10 pm. Plan your day such that Anushka's dad could go to pick her up from the party instead of allowing her to travel alone.

PARENTING Tip

Instead of tightening the noose, allow enough freedom to the children so that they do not feel suffocated. Keep a close eye on them initially because they may be ill-equipped to handle the freedom in the beginning, then loosen your hold slowly.

FB Fiasco

FB, Twitter, Google+, etc. are some of the popular social networking sites which are the craze among the youth today. But they are not as much in the good books of the parents.

Are the parents being the old duck or are their younglings overdoing this SNS bit?

Arjun lives in Chandigarh. He is like a normal youth of today whose life revolves around various networking sites. He has his own group of friends in school and an even bigger group of friends on Facebook. He loves interacting with them and spends a better part of his day on Internet. Let's meet Arjun and his family and see what they feel in this matter.

Members in Arjun's family

Arjun - 19 years old (student of class XII)
Surinder Ahuja – Arjun's father (self-employed, runs a grocery shop)
Radha – Arjun's mother (housewife)
Neha – Arjun's sister (16 years old, student of class X)

THE CONFLICT!!!

You are again on FB. When will you complete your assignment?

Papa, this is my assignment.

Arjun's Diary

Monday, February 2, nightfall

Papa again shouted at me for not studying and wasting my time on Facebook. But I was studying! Why does he blow his top every time he sees me on computer?

It is not my fault that he cannot understand the ABC of computers. I have tried it so many times but he cannot get the hang of it. Most of my friends' parents are on Facebook. They know what it is like and they do not mind them spending some time chatting with their friends.

But my father works with a single track mind. For him, something is either bad or good. There cannot be a middle route. He thinks that when I am sitting on computer and I have Facebook open then I am only talking rubbish with my friends.

I agree, we do have our fun, but along with that we do other things also. Like the other day, I completed my chemistry project with inputs from my friends on Facebook. We were chatting online and I could do all the additions and changes as if we were doing it together.

We all had to submit that project the next day and there was no way we could do it together without raising too many suspicious eyes (read parents) who do not understand the concept of group study either.

I flunked my XII grade last year and it has been completely blamed on my Facebook addiction. This is not true. The truth is that I had chicken pox just before my physics exam and could not study properly. But he wouldn't listen to any reason when he is in the mood to put blame on something for my failure.

From unlimited access to computer now, I have only very limited time on computer. Even that time, Papa wants to alter. He would have completely cut me off the computer, if I did not have Informatics Practice as one of my main subjects.

He does the same even with Neha, who cries and simply gives in at such times. She has even deleted her Facebook account. But I am not a fool like her. I am not going to allow him to cut me off from the world like this. My friends would laugh at me if I tell them that I am off Facebook.

I wish my father was reasonable enough to discuss these issues with me.

1. What is wrong with visiting the social networking sites? Don't we socialise in our family and friends circle too?
2. Why does he always feel that I am wasting my time on Facebook?
3. Why does he not learn and open his own account like other parents on Facebook? Maybe then he can understand me better.
4. What is the need to link my flunking the boards last year with my Facebook account?
5. If I want to be updated and in sync with my times, then what is wrong in it?

I wish Papa would read my mind and give me answers to all the above questions which have been haunting me.

Arjun

Counsellor Speaks

The problem between Arjun and his father is not just the difference of opinion, but it is also not understanding each other's viewpoint.

For Parents

- Arjun is at such a crucial stage when too much nagging may turn him into a rebel. So do not constantly pester him to study. It's true that he should spend the major part of his day in studying but let him enjoy a chat for half an hour, twice a day. You may set the time frame for him and let him adhere to it. Do not give him free access to Internet all the time.
- You may not have any inclination or time to join a social networking site, but occasionally, you may sit with your son and see how it works and learn from him.
- Do not bring up the topic of paying fees for repeated year or say any such thing which may hurt the pride of your child. Teenagers tend to absorb such things more easily and hold the grouse in their hearts for a long time.

Parenting Tip

Change with the era and grow up with your kids in their times. Do not let terms like generation gap come into your relationship with your children. The love between parents and children is beyond time, it is only the conditions around them which make it seem like a tough battle. So instead of looking at all their activities suspiciously from afar, join them.

Hole in My Pocket

While children like their pockets to be full all the time, parents worry that extra money may spoil the children.

Pocket money or no pocket money! This is one question which bothers both parents and kids alike, though for different reasons.

Meet Rajat and his father who have opposing views on the matter. Rajat lives in Delhi. He and his friends frequent nearby malls and have fun. This requires money and most of the time, Rajat somehow manages. But there are times when he gets stuck and feels embarrassed.

Members in Rajat's family :

Rajat – 16-year-old boy (student of class XI)
Tilak Singh- Rajat's father (bank employee)
Subhadra – Rajat's mother (school teacher)
Abhinav – Rajat's brother (9-year old)

THE CONFLICT!!!

Rajat's Diary

Saturday, March 22, evening

I wish to hide in a corner as I recall today's incident. After the final exams, my group decided to go to the nearby mall and have lunch at KFC (Kentucky Fried Chicken). I went ahead with them as I was sure that there was enough cash in my wallet to cover my lunch. (we always go dutch on such outings.) During the lunch, everyone was in such a good mood that everyone decided to go and watch the latest movie in the nearby PVR theatre. I tried my best to chicken out because I knew that I did not have enough cash but no one would listen to me. While buying the tickets, they had to chip in to buy my ticket as I did not have any spare cash in my wallet. I felt like a beggar. I wanted to die of embarrassment.

My father earns enough for a family of four. My mother is a working woman too. Still when it comes to giving me my pocket money, they turn such misers. They would spend thousands on my books, clothes and various other things but when it comes to hand me cash as pocket money, they treat me like a toddler who does not know how to keep his money.

Imagine giving a measly thousand bucks a month to a teenage boy in this era. My friends get unlimited amount to spend. One or two even have their own credit cards. But my parents wouldn't give me a single penny more than my pocket money.

I wanted to work during my vacations so that I could earn some extra bucks. I even got an offer to work for fifteen days at a stall in IITF during November, but papa refused.

I feel like a destitute sometimes, begging to them for money. Even I would like to do some shopping on my own like last month when I wanted to buy a beautiful coffee maker for mom's birthday, but could not do so because I did not have enough money. When I asked for an advance on my pocket money from papa, he refused to do so. I did not want to let go of that coffee maker so I took out money from mummy's bag without telling her. I managed to gift her that coffee maker but soon my theft was discovered and I was branded as thief by papa. I felt so stuck up. I wanted to run away. But where and how?

I wish I could make my parents understand my predicament and discuss these issues with them.

1. Why can I not get enough pocket money when my friends get from their parents?

2. If my parents cannot increase my allowance then why should they not allow me to work part time?

3. Why does papa call me thief when I only once took out some money from my mother's wallet without asking her?

I wish papa understands my feelings and does not misinterpret my actions.

Rajat

Counsellor Speaks

Rajat and his father agree that Rajat should get pocket money, but they have totally different views when it comes to the amount of pocket money he should get.

For Parents

- ❐ Instead of just handing over the cash to Rajat every month, sit with him once in a while and make him understand how he can spend some money and how he can save a part of his pocket money. Budgeting, saving and spending are all required to be understood while tackling money.
- ❐ While dealing with Rajat, you should keep in mind that he is not a grown up man, but just a teenager. You should not be so rigid with him. If he had the confidence in you, he would not have stolen money from his mother's wallet. You should not deny him outrightly any demand that he places before you.
- ❐ Do not brand him a thief. Remember Rajat did not steal money to watch a movie, he did this out of necessity. He wanted to buy a gift for his mother.

Parenting Tip

Money holds a place of prime importance in this material world. But the confidence you give your child to depend upon you in any circumstances is invaluable.

At Your Desk...

Studies are important in life. But is it necessary to spend most of the time to study or should there be a balance in studies and other activities? To answer this question, let us meet Sujata's family.

Sujata lives in Dehradun. Her mother is a single parent so she feels all the more responsible for her children. This makes her act unreasonably strict and sometimes even depresses her. This depression spreads to all the family members and the environment in the house becomes very suffocating.

There are three members in Sujata's family:

Sujata – 15-year-old girl (student of class IX)
Radhika Biyani – Sujata's mother (a government employee)
Gopal – Sujata's brother (18-year old student of class XII)

THE CONFLICT!!!

Sujata's Diary

Wednesday, January 27, morning

Thank goodness. Mummy has gone to office. Yesterday was such a nightmare. It was Republic Day holiday and mummy was at home. I got up around nine and woke up Gopal too. We both sat down before the television the moment Republic Day parade began. As it is, we hardly watch any TV programme, thanks to mummy who refuses to take a cable connection or a dish. Both of us were planning to watch this parade till the end and then go and study. We did not even wake up mummy hoping that she will get up late and will not stop us from watching the programme.

But right in the middle of the parade, at around 10:45, mummy came and stood before us. We tried to pacify her and come to an understanding that the moment this parade ended, we would go and study but she would have none of it. First, she scolded Gopal left and right for not studying even though he had his board practical exam on the 27th. Reluctantly, Gopal went into his room to study. Then she turned to me. She blamed me for pulling Gopal into this. How lame can that be? Is Gopal a little child who can be coaxed into doing something that would harm his career? In any case, it was just a practical exam and he was going to study soon after the parade was over.

Her harsh words made me cry and I too ran into my room. Soon we both had our books open in front of us, but it was hours before we could concentrate.

Mummy can be very unreasonable at times. She does not understand us at all. She is still living in the times when parents considered it their duty to reprimand their children for everything. Times have changed. I feel today's generation is much more responsible. Then what is the need of being so strict with us? It does not serve any purpose, rather it makes us find ways to escape this unnecessary argument. If we ever say something, she starts wallowing in self-pity of being a single parent and how she misses papa. Don't we all miss him?

Many a time when I do not feel like studying, I just open a story book within my course book and sit on my table. When mummy sees me from afar she feels that I have my course book open in front of me. She looks satisfied and does not come and check. This has been going on for quite some time and she never got a hint of it. But last week, I did this ploy and as luck would have it, I went to attend a phone call leaving my books on the table as it is. Mummy came into my room for some work at that time and she saw that I was reading a story book under my course book. All hell broke loose. I got a good scolding and almost got thrashed for being such a cheat. I wanted to say sorry to her. I wanted to make her understand my situation but I am so scared of her wrath that I feel tongue tied in front of her. Even Gopal feels the same.

I wish she would understand us better so these things which are troubling me would not bother me so much.

1. Why does she not let us take responsibility of our life?
2. Why is she so strict that we cannot even talk to her normally?
3. Why does she think that by sitting on our table and keeping our books open in front of us, we will become geniuses?
4. Why does she always want us to pity her for being a single parent? We also miss our father so much.

I wish papa was there to understand our feelings.

Sujata

Counsellor Speaks

Studies form a major bone of contention between parents and children. While parents want their kids glued to their books and tables, children want their own space and freedom to do things their own way.

For Parents

- ☐ Children feel suffocated if they are not given enough freedom to do as they like. You know the level of intelligence of your children. Compare it with the results they are getting and decide the course of action based on this fact. Do not expect moon from your children. Let them grow normally.
- ☐ If you have suffered your husband's loss, so have the children who miss their father. So never try to emotionally blackmail them on this front.
- ☐ Sitting on the desk with book open in front will not help in studying. Let them study as much and whenever Sujata and Gopal want to. Once they understand their responsibility and do not feel pressurised, they will perform better.
- ☐ In today's hi-tech age, it is important to be connected and aware. You cannot shut off your children from the world by not allowing them to watch TV or sit on Internet or go out with friends once in a while. So loosen your stand. Instead of being a strict parent, just be their friend and see how they will sit on their desk without your reminding them.

PARENTING Tip

Have faith in the abilities of your children. As a parent you may show them the right path. How far they follow it entirely depends upon them.

Remote Control

These days our main source of entertainment is television. After a day's hard work, everyone wants to just relax at home and gear up for the next day. In such a scenario, 'who holds the remote…' may turn into a fight for power.

Vineet lives in Nagpur. In their lower middle class family, television is the only source of entertainment. Unlike other households, there is only one television set in his house and everyone has different tastes when it comes to watching programmes.

The members in Bhardwaj family:

Vineet – 19 years old (college student)
Mahendra Bhardwaj – Vineet's father (a government employee)
Sudha Bhardwaj – Vineet's mother (housewife)
Shashank and Shreya – Vineet's twin brother and sister duo (study in class VII)

THE CONFLICT!!!

Dad, it's the first ODI between India and Australia!

So what? The game is over. They are showing the highlights.

Vineet's Diary

Sunday, April 26, midnight

Today was such a bad day. The Indian cricket team lost today's ODI match against Australia. I believe they put up a tough fight, but unfortunately, I could'nt see the entire match. I had completed my assignments during the day so that I was free to watch the highlights of the match which would go on till late at night. Just as the match was getting interesting, dad came and took the remote from me. He switched the channels and settled down with news bulletin. The results of by-elections in our state were being declared today. I tried to coax him into letting me see the match that was far more interesting than his boring elections, but he would not listen to me. He told me to go and study in my room.

I felt so helpless. I could have gone to my friend's house to watch the match but that was also not allowed as it was a late night match. After he was through with his news, mummy came and put on some boring Film Awards which seemed to go on forever. Remote shifted hands but it never reached me. In the meanwhile, the match finished.

Oh this is so irritating. I have asked him so many times to at least get me another television set on which I could watch my favourite programmes but he refuses to relent. There is only one television set for the entire family and the remote keeps changing hands as if it was a power game of politics.

'More TV sets means less studies' is his motto. Mummy also seconds him. She won't understand my problem. She has the remote for herself the whole day. Whatever programme she misses in the evening, she can catch up in the re-runs during the day. Shreya and Shashank are happy enough to watch just anything so long as they can skip their books and sit in front of TV. I come home around five in the evening from college and within an hour, dad is also back. Then begins the real tussle of the remote. I would not mind watching TV with him but he watches such boring programmes.

Last Monday, I was watching a very interesting episode of Supernatural serial. During the break, I went inside to fetch something. When I came back, he had already changed the channel and sat there holding the remote securely. I requested him to let me finish my half-seen serial, but he refused to hand over the remote to me. During the commercial breaks, he relented, but unfortunately, all the commercial breaks come at the same time. I got so angry that I stormed out of the room.

To even the scores, a day later, I did the same with him when he went to attend a phone call in the next room during a break. I switched channels and held on to the remote in the same manner as he did that day. But lo and behold! He came back and snatched the remote from me and switched to his favourite programme and resumed watching. I tried to protest but a stern look from him forced me to shut up and coop up in my room.

Such double standards! But whom to complain?

No one in the house understands my problem. They somehow manage to agree on a common programme and enjoy it. But I want the remote in my hand and want to watch TV as per my wish.

I would like to ask dad these three questions.

1. Why does he think that remote of the TV is his property? Are we not fellow human beings who have the same rights in the house as he has?
2. Why should dad scold me for nicking the remote from him during his favourite programme when he himself does the same with me?
3. Is my demand for a separate television set so outrageous that daddy does not even give it a thought?

Vineet

Counsellor Speaks

When life becomes a series of battles over such a trivial thing like remote then it's time to rethink your actions.

For Parents

- All these years you have enjoyed the freedom of showing the right path to your children. Now also you need not give in to their unjust demands just for the sake of it.
- However, being so rigid in your stance may not be good for your relationship with your teenaged son. You must learn to relent and give in to him sometimes. Once in a while, you should allow him to watch his programmes on television rather than always forcing him to watch what you feel right. He will feel bullied if you do this all the time and soon, he will rebel.

Parenting Tip

It is very childish to compete with your own children in holding the remote control of the television. Demonstrate some maturity and do not indulge in such tactics.

Set Me Free

Everyone likes to live like a free bird. But there is a thin line between living a free life and living a frivolous life. If we flaunt the norms of the society, ignore our duties and live selfishly then it is wrong.

Pranav lives in Panipat. He has a loving family. His sister Pragati loves him very much and tries to protect him whenever required. But Pranav does not come upto everyone's expectations. He seem to have gone off his rockers due to the failures that have led to his frustration.

Let's meet Pranav and his family:

Pranav – 19 years old (repeating class XII)
Pragati – 19 years old twin of Pranav (in college)
Charanjit Singh – Father (owner of a banquet hall)
Shalini Singh – Mother (housewife)
Pragya and Puja – Elder sisters (both married)
Dada and Dadi – Grandfather and Grandmother

THE CONFLICT!!!

Pranab wants to live a free life. He does'nt like to take orders from anyone.

Pranav's Sister, Pragati's Diary

Sunday, July 26, midnight

Pranav hasn't come back yet. I don't know what to do. I have to go to college tomorrow early. I wish he would come back soon, so that I can open the gate for him and then catch some sleep.

Papa is out of town and everyone else thinks that Pranav is sleeping in his room. I do not like to deceive everyone like this, but sometimes, I feel pity on Pranav and then I let him have his way.

This has become a norm for quite some time. I have been covering up for him for so many other things too. Pranav wants to live a free life. He does not like to take orders from anyone. But there are so many things which bind him to the home front. First of all, he is the only son, so naturally, everyone is extra worried about his safety.

Although, I feel he has become quite a brat because of extra attention showered on him by amma, dada and dadi. Being the only son, they have given him too much liberty. Only papa knows how to rein him, but he too goes overboard. While amma, dadi and dada are too lenient, papa is too strict with him.

However, papa also indulges him. Pranav has always got whatever he wanted. But now papa has realised that this is making him rude and irresponsible. I remember last year when Pranav wanted to have a bike, the whole family refused. Papa refused because he was afraid that Pranav would neglect his studies and others were worried about his safety. Fuming he refused to ride his bicycle and ended up having to go to school on foot.

Later, when Pranav flunked in class XII, papa became all the more strict. Now he does not even allow Pranav to go for movies, discos or even to malls. I agree that if Pranav had studied hard, he would have scraped through and would not have been repeating a year. But that does not mean he should be denied of all his freedom.

There are a few questions that come to my mind.

1. Is your grade in exams the only criteria to allow or disallow your freedom?
2. Why does everyone treat Pranav like a puppet and expect him to do their bidding?
3. Does Pranav not have his own will?
4. Can't Pranav be allowed his space and freedom?

Pragati

Counsellor Speaks

Today's teenagers are very sensitive. They feel strongly about their surroundings, people and actions.

For Parents
- Times are changing and children are not as obedient as were the norms some time ago. It is better if you give in to the wishes of your children once in a while.
- What seriously lacks between you and your son is a dialogue. Give words to your feelings and make him understand why you are denying him some privileges which he feels he should get.

Parenting Tip

Demonstrate your love for your children through understanding and gestures and not by things that you buy for them.

What Do I Care!

Sharing and caring are part of a family. Life becomes much more enjoyable when you know there is someone who cares.

Amitav lives in Gurgaon. His family is affluent and they lead a rich lifestyle. However, at times, Amitav misses the love and affection of a loving family despite all the money his parents give him.

Let's meet the Mittal family:

Amitav – 13 years old (student of class VII)
Ranjan Mittal – Amitav's father (successful businessman)
Saroj – Amitav's mother (housewife and socialite)

THE CONFLICT!!!

Amitav's Diary

Sunday, June 2, pre-noon

I am feeling terrible. I have been down with fever for the past three days. Today the fever has come down but I feel very sick. In the morning also, I woke up feeling sick and my head was hurting as if someone was banging hammers on it. I was throwing up in the washroom when mom came into my room. She was all dressed to go somewhere. She heard me in the washroom but did not come there. 'Are you okay, Amit.' was all she said. I grunted. 'I am going for my kitty party. Tell maid whatever you want for lunch. Bye.' And she was off in a jiffy. Though I am used to living alone, I wish there was someone to be with me when I am ill. Since childhood, I have been looked after by the maids. Mom was always too busy with her kitty parties and social gatherings. It seems her duty was over after she delivered me in the hands of the maids.

I see my friends, who have doting parents who look after them all the time. My parents are hardly ever at home. Dad is always busy in his work and mom with her social life. Earlier, she was not like this but now she does not care about me at all. She has created a social circle for herself in which I am most unwanted.

I used to crave for their company initially, but now it seems I have hardened up and do not feel anything for them. To me, they are more like my providers than parents.

Last month, mom came down with viral attack. She was in bed for two days. Even the maid was on leave those days. But I felt no inclination to go to her room and soothe her. When she has never done such a thing, why should I? Instead I went to my friend's place and spent the whole day there. When I came back late in the night, I could see from her face that she was upset but it gave me certain inner satisfaction, something like settling the scores.

Ruchit, my friend, also told me one day that he heard his mother talking that my dad had left us for another woman and that is why he is mostly not around. But I don't trust him. If there was some such thing, my mom would have told me. I know dad is mostly away on tours.

I really wish to ask my parents a few questions.

1. Why did you bring me into this world if you were not ready to take the responsibility?
2. Why do you feel bad when I do not care for you because I have learnt this from you?
3. Why is it that the parents of other children care for them all the time, whereas none of you ever do?

Amitav

Counsellor Speaks

Sometimes, what we see is not entirely true. There may be hidden facts behind it which unfold before us when the time is appropriate.

For Parents

- ☐ The troubles you face in your marital life is your own. Your child should not suffer because of this. Since you have decided on a kind of pact and are not separating for the sake of your son, then it becomes your duty to provide him with the loving family environment.
- ☐ You should sit together and find a way so that Amitav does not have to face a depressed, neglected childhood. It is as much the duty of the father as that of the mother to give a good upbringing to your child.

Parenting Tip

We all face ups and downs in our lives, but becoming insensitive towards our loved ones does not solve the problem. In fact, it is the love and affection of our beloved people that gives us the strength to come out of any storm unscathed.

Attitude Problem

The modern generation or gen Y, as they are called, is quite straightforward. They speak their mind and do not hesitate in making their thoughts vocal.

Sanyukta lives in Delhi. She is a headstrong girl. But sometimes, her stubborn attitude crosses the limits and upsets her parents. Let's meet the Saxena family.

> **There are four members in the Saxena family:**
>
> Sanyukta – 19 years old (Doing first year in college)
> Sanjay Saxena – Sanyukta's father (a government employee)
> Vandana Saxena – Sanyukta's mother (housewife)
> Sanjeev – Sanyukta's brother (an MBA student)

THE CONFLICT!!!

Sanyukta's Diary

Friday, May 5, midnight

Oh my God! Mummy is so irritating. She is so old-fashioned. She has to know everything, and for that she continues to poke her nose into everything. She hails from a village and even though, she has done her graduation, she is living in ancient times.

She can't bear to see me wearing modern clothes. She does not like my going to college on bike with boys. She seems to have problem with everything I do.

I can't bear such dictatorship and retaliate when the situation seems to go out of hand.

In the morning as I was leaving for college, she started off again. She did not want me to go to college in spaghetti top. Now I can't go to college in salwar kameez. She would not listen while Ronit was waiting outside on his bike. I had no choice but to snub her and leave.

Though papa is not so strict and he understands the changing times, but when it comes to choose between me and mummy, he sides with her. Last week, when we were going on a picnic, she kept asking me about who all were going. Then she kept on calling me on my mobile. This made me a laughing stock before my friends. Ultimately, I had to switch off my mobile. And as expected, I came home to a hyper-anxious mother pacing up and down. Lucky, I did not give her my friends' mobile numbers; else she would have been calling them all. I had a big fight with mummy that day.

I wonder what she wants from me. She lectures me on being good, doing something for the society, etc., and when I went to join the Anna Hazare's movement at the Red Fort, she got jeepers.

I wish I could ask mummy these three questions.

1. *Why does she behave in such old-fashioned manner?*
2. *Why does she think that she possesses me? Why can't she let me be myself?*
3. *Why does she think I am rude when I am merely stating my views?*

Sanyukta

Counsellor Speaks

In our country, as technology has taken a big leap, so has the culture. The soft-spoken manner of yesteryears is gone and a straightforward approach has taken over.

For Parents

- Over the years, you have gained experience and patience. Now is the time to exercise it. Your daughter is passing that phase which may make her feel that she owns the life. In her enthusiasm, she may appear rude and defiant. But do not lose heart and bear with her. She will come around soon.
- You are doing the right thing by keeping a close eye on the activities of your daughter but if you overdo it and start distrusting her on all fronts, then it may lead to misapprehensions and misunderstandings. So have trust in her and keep an eye on her from afar. Give her some freedom and see how she comes back to you to tie the love bonds.

Parenting Tip

As children enter the world, they want to fly like a free bird. It is your duty to teach them to fly in the right direction. Do not feel perturbed with their arrogance and attitude; it's a passing phase which will soon be over.

Dating Blues

Dating is not a new concept in our society now, yet it evokes mixed feelings in parents. Some fear it, some dread it, some simply abhor it. But one thing is sure, they cannot ignore it.

Rachna lives in Kanpur. She is a modern girl who believes that friendship between girls and boys is normal. However, her parents think otherwise. Let's meet Rachna's parents and see what they think about it.

There are four members in Rachna's family:

Rachna – 15-years old teenager (studying in class XI)
Ritu – Rachna's mother (a school teacher)
Raman Chaturvedi – Rachna's father (a police inspector)
Richa – Rachna's sister (recently married)

THE CONFLICT!!!

Rachna's Diary

Saturday, October 14, midnight

What a terrible day. I am so exhausted both mentally and physically. It all started when my classmate Robin asked me to go with him on a date. He is the handsome hunk of our class and I could not in my wildest dreams imagine him asking me for a date. I immediately said, yes. We fixed it up for today. I was to meet him near the Plaza Mall.

I was very excited. I did not tell my parents; naturally, they wouldn't understand this concept of dating. They are so strict and orthodox. Only my best friend Kritika knew about it.

I met Robin around twelve noon. Then we went to Subway to grab a bite. Then Robin took me to a nearby garden and we sat under a tree in the warm sun laughing and talking. It was so much fun till it lasted. Then suddenly a heavy hand fell on my shoulder and someone grabbed Robin from behind. My first reaction was that some unruly characters were grabbing me and kidnapping me. But when I turned around I saw two female police constables standing there. They abused us. When Robin tried to defend us, one of them slapped him hard on his face. They asked us to sit in the police jeep and took us to the nearby police station. It seems there was some police drive going on in which they caught couples from the parks and punished them for creating obscenity in public places. We pleaded saying that we were classmates and we were just sitting there talking to each other, and this was the truth. But they simply laughed it aside. Their manner was so humiliating. I wanted to hide under the ground.

But this was not the end of it. When we were taken inside the police station, I found myself standing before our family friend, Kadir chacha who was posted as the inspector at this police station. I didn't know where to look. For no fault of mine, I was facing this disgrace.

I wanted to call papa but what would I do if he reprimanded me in front of everyone.

The events that follow are much a blur in my memory. Kadir chacha called up my father on his own, who came there soon. The matter was hushed up then and there, much to the relief of Robin. But I had much to face. Papa took me home. On the way, he did not speak a word to me. Once inside the house, he scolded me right and left. When mummy got to know of all this, she gave me one tight slap. After much shouts and cries, the house became quiet. I had locked myself in my room. But for how long! Sooner or later, I had to face them.

I wanted to ask my parents the following things, but did not have the courage.

1. *Can someone please tell me what was my fault that I had to suffer so much trauma?*

2. *Why couldn't papa and mummy understand that times have changed and there is nothing wrong with dating?*

3. *How will I face my friends in school when they will get to know of this incident?*

Rachna

Counsellor Speaks

Life is not always a bed of roses. Sometimes situation becomes so tricky that it requires clever handling of the matter.

For Parents
- ❏ The fear instilled in Rachna's mind did not allow her to confide in any of you before going out or even call one of you from the police station. This happens when the child does not have trust in the parents. It is this trust that you should instill in her. She should understand that you are there for her at all times.
- ❏ You should have more communication with Rachna. This way she will be able to express herself freely and fearlessly before you.
- ❏ You should make her understand the realities of life. She is still very young and does not know the complexities of social norms. It is for you to instill the right values in her at this moment.

Parenting Tip
Sometimes teenagers create a block in their minds which stops them from reaching out to their parents. It is the duty of the parents to resolve this by taking the first step.

Gymming

Being health conscious is good but losing weight on account of food phobia is not healthy.

Let us meet Sadhika who had to face such a problem. Sadhika got carried away by the new fad of being size zero and went on crash dieting. This adversely affected her health. Now she is in a quandary.

Let's meet Sadhika and her family:

Sadhika – 19 years old college student
Sonu – Sadhika's mother, a dietician
Jiten Mansukhani – Sadhika's father, garment exporter
Sujit – Sadhika's 15-year-old brother

THE CONFLICT!!!

Sadhika's Diary

Wednesday, August, 19, midnight

Today is my birthday. I had invited all my friends for dinner and then we planned to go out for ice cream. But nothing goes as per planned. I wore my new red dress. I know I was looking pretty after having lost all that flab. I was basking in the glory of being size zero.

The party began with a zing. We were all dancing and singing. When the servant brought in starters, everyone had them with a gusto. I took one bite in the spring roll and my stomach lurched.

However, much I wanted to, I just couldn't eat beyond that one bite. When food was served, I again tried to eat, but soon after, I felt sick and had to throw up.

Although this has been going on for quite some time, but today, I really felt bad. Because of this, I could not enjoy my birthday.

When everyone left, I told my mother how the smell or thought of food was making me sick. She scolded me for not paying attention to my health. Earlier also, she had warned me that I was overdoing this dieting bit by spending the whole day on nimbu-pani. That time I did not listen to her and felt happy in my new-found slim and trim figure. Its aftereffects are now showing. I don't know what to do.

I wonder why this is happening to me. All my college friends are slim. They are not size zero, but they are not as fat either as I used to be. They never have this problem. They eat everything under the sun.

I want to ask my mother:

1. Why did she allow me to put on so much weight initially when she herself is a dietician?

2. Why did she not stop me forcefully when I went on crash dieting?

3. Why did she give me such genes that I put on weight so easily?

Sadhika

Counsellor Speaks

Anorexia nervosa is a disease in which the person is afraid of eating. This aversion to food gets instilled in the mind of the person who is dieting for a long time.

For Parents

- ☐ Your daughter is suffering from an ailment which can be cured by proper treatment. Do not give in to her whims and fancies and get her treated at your earliest.
- ☐ If she does not listen to her mother, the father should intervene and make her understand the importance of health in life.
- ☐ You may even take help of her friends because at this age peer pressure is at its peak.

PARENTING Tip

In their urge to be a part of their group, teenagers imitate others and try to become the fashion icons. This sometimes proves too hard on their health.

Mobile Mania

There was a time when telephone was a luxury. Today mobile phones have entered the market and they have become a necessity of life.

Shambhavi lives in Hyderabad. As a sign of affluence and modernisation, each one in her family owns a mobile. If the mobile has been considered an important tool for communication, then the family takes it literally and they are on their respective mobiles most of the time. So much so that conversation among themselves has dwindled to monosyllables.

Let's meet Shambhavi and her family:

Shambhavi – daughter (18-year-old college student)
Malti – mother (a boutique owner)
Ravi Prasad – father (import-export business)
Arjun – Shambhavi's 16-year-old brother

THE CONFLICT!!!

Shambhavi's Diary

Thursday, February 12, Nightfall

Two days later is the Valentine's Day, Adi called me in the evening to fix a date. I was talking to him on my mobile when daddy's mobile began to ring. He picked up the phone and started talking so loudly that I could hardly hear a word that Adi was saying. I went to my bedroom, but there Arjun was taking some notes from his friend, again on his mobile. I went to the balcony near the kitchen and what do I find, mummy talking to her client loudly on her mobile.

For a moment, I felt like laughing at the irony of the situation. Four people in our small happy family and all four of us were talking on our respective mobiles. It was as if four paying guests were living in a guest house.

The worst thing was that Adi got cheesed off and disconnected the call.

I tried to call him but by that time, daddy had finished his call and when he saw me still on my mobile, he began to scold me.

I would like to ask him this:

1. Why me? When mummy and Arjun were also doing the same and for that matter, a few moments ago, he too was talking on his mobile, then why single me out?

2. Secondly, he keeps harping about this family thing that we should spend quality time together. However, in our house most of the time everyone is talking on their respective mobiles, then what quality time is he talking about?

3. When his calls come, he picks up the mobile on priority and talks on it for hours, but when my call comes, he has no respect for the caller, and as soon as he notices me talking on my mobile, he would start shouting at me. Isn't this unfair?

Shambhavi

Counsellor Speaks

Mobiles may be a boon, but there is a dark side too. For those, who value their time with the family, the mobile may prove to be a hamper.

For Parents

- ☐ You should remember that children do what they see their parents do. So if you want your children to switch off their mobiles during meals then both of you should first follow this practice, however hard it may seem.

- ☐ Directing someone's anger at another person is not a good practice. In fact, it is better not to scold your teenaged children. Make them understand with love and care; they will surely understand your point of view.

PARENTING Tip

If the mobile that connects you to the world, starts alienating you from your family then it is time to reconsider the way you use this gadget.

Tag Along

Parents and children together make a family. Till the children are small, the entire family goes together to each and every function. But once these kids enter their teens, they begin to exercise their likes and dislikes.

Abhijit's parents believe that they should always be seen as a family whether it is a marriage function or a party. They want their children to know their roots and relatives. But in this quest, they go a little overboard ignoring the urgencies and emergencies of children which may bind them from time to time.

Let's meet Abhijit and his family:

Abhijit – 16 years old (student of class X)
Rajendra Vajpayee – Abhijit's father (government job)
Sonika – Abhijit's mother (housewife)
Shikha – Abhijit's 13-year-old sister (student of class VIII)

THE CONFLICT!!!

Abhijit's Diary

Wednesday, December 17, nightfall

Sometimes mom and dad act so irrationally. Mom's distant cousin's daughter is getting married tonight. Without asking me, mom and dad had assumed that we would all go together. But this time, I had to put my foot down. I point blankly refused to go with them as tag along. I hardly know those people.

I would just go there and stand with a smile pasted on my face. Oh I hate such gatherings. Even Shikha feels the same, but she is too scared to say all this to mom or dad. My parents should understand that we have grown up now. Gone are the days when we would tag behind them like a puppy. Now we have our own life, our own schedule and our own group of people with whom we like to mingle. Why, then force us to accompany them when it is not so important? I don't mind going to such functions, where I know people and I do enjoy meeting them.

The same thing happened last month too. There was a wedding in the family. As usual, it was assumed that all of us will be going for the wedding despite the fact that I had my physics exam the next day. Normally, none of us go for a function if any of us has some pressing assignment, but this time both mom and dad were like I could study for the exam beforehand. I tried to make them understand that the syllabus was vast and I needed more time, but they paid no heed. So I went there sulking. The next day's paper was a disaster and I got very poor marks in physics.

I would like to ask my parents:

1. Why is it important for them that wherever they go, we should go together?

2. When would our parents understand that we are grown up individuals?

3. Why do they insist on taking us with them when we do not even know those people whom we are forced to meet?

4. How would they feel if we forced them to come to our parties?

5. Are they not giving undue importance to such parties?

Abhijit

Counsellor Speaks

There is a clear difference in opinion between two generations. Both are right in their own thinking, so it is better to come to an agreement by taking a middle path.

For Parents

- ❏ Your views about teaching your children the art of socialising is commendable, but you should keep in mind that your children are growing up now. So give them their time and space.
- ❏ Living as a family and going out together is a good thought. So long as it does not hamper the activities of other members, it should be followed. But too much rigidity may be harmful for relationships. So be flexible in your approach.
- ❏ If you feel that family outings are less and you manage to get quality family time only at functions, then it is time for you to reconsider your living style. Arrange picnics and more outings with your family so that you do not feel the need to go out together every time even at the expense of someone's important work suffering because of that.

Parenting Tip

Allow space to your children. They are growing up and as they have become familiar with your social circle, they are building their own social group too. So do not think that they are incapable of socialising. Let them be on their own once in a while.

My Friends...Your Friends

We all like to spend time with our friends. But when the parents try to mingle with the friends of their children, then it may not be to the liking of all.

Let's meet Saumya's family. She lives in Indore. She belongs to an upper middle class family. Her parents are well educated and modern. Both her mother and father have jobs which keep them occupied from morning till evening. Being an only child of working parents, Saumya spends most of her time with her friends.

Let's meet Saumya and her parents:

Saumya— 18-year-old college student
Ruchika – Saumya's mother, works as a receptionist
Sachin Srivastava – Saumya's father (a government employee)

THE CONFLICT!!!

Saumya's Diary

Sunday, June 19, midnight

Whew, what a day!

Today was Sunday, so I and my friends decided to go for a movie. It was decided that they would all assemble at my house. There were five girls and two boys. They all reached on time. I was a little late in getting ready. So they sat with my parents. And it was the same story all over again. When I came out, I found my mother and father laughing and joking with my friends as if they too were teenagers. I found it so embarrassing. It seemed my friends were enjoying because I had to pull them all out on the pretext of missing the movie. One or two even had the gall to invite my parents to come for the movie with us. It was so irritating. I confronted them after I came back from the movie, but they do not seem to understand. It always begins with my trying to make them see reason, and with mom and dad sulking in their rooms later.

This is not the first time this type of thing happened. On many earlier occasions, mom would come and steal my time with my friends. I know she is prettier than me and much more fun-loving, but why must she try to flirt with everyone? Why can't she leave us alone? It goes the same for dad as well.

What do they think? They are still as young as they were thirty years ago? When I go to my friends' houses I notice how their parents behave with us. They just nod to us when we wish them and then go back to their own chores. They do not try to mingle with our lot. I would die of embarrassment if they sit with me and ask me a hundred and ten questions.

The same thing happened on my birthday party. Very reluctantly, I invited my friends last year to my house for my birthday party. I made sure that they stayed clear of the party. I told mom to go and watch TV in her room after making all the arrangements for the party, so that I could have free time with my friends. But as we were dancing together, someone went inside and brought her out, and they made her sing a song. Then she danced with us. Later that night, I had a fight with her. She tried to placate me by saying that it was my friends who forced her to come out. It left me fuming. Okay, but then who asked her to sing that song? She is not a small kid that someone could force something out of her.

Since then I stopped calling my friends over. I rather go to their house or we meet somewhere outside. If at all I call them, it is when my parents are not there.

I would like to ask my parents these things-

1. Why can't they act their age while talking to my friends?

2. Why can't they mingle with their own group and leave mine alone?

3. Don't they see how my friends detest their presence amidst us?

4. How would they feel if I start sitting with their friends and talking to them as if I was their age?

Saumya

Counsellor Speaks

Teenagers lack maturity of thought and may look at a situation differently from elders. It is the duty of the parents to handle such situations tactfully without hurting the teens.

For Parents

- You should try to work on the complex that Saumya has because she feels her mother is a step ahead from her in beauty and other fields. Help her to inculcate some hobbies which highlight her hidden talent.
- On your part, you may avoid going and talking to her friends most times. Ultimately, they are your daughter's friends and if she is not very comfortable with your overly interaction with them, then you may cut it and simply be courteous to them rather than being overfriendly.
- Finally, it is important to make Saumya understand that she has no right to snub you or talk to you disrespectfully before anyone. Being an only child does not mean she can take advantage of the situation and demean you. Be firm and take a strict stance.

Parenting Tip
Sometimes looking at a situation from your children's perspective gives you an entirely different view.

Dressing Spells Doom

Over the years, everyone's dressing style changes. How you dress as a child changes as you turn into a teenager. Similarly, as you grow in life and climb the ladder in social circle, your style of dressing changes accordingly.

Sometimes parents forget that they are not appropriately dressed for their age and this may cause embarrassment for their offsprings.

Let's meet Rishabh who lives with his family in the cosmopolitan city of Mumbai. His father dresses in the modern clothes and at times tries to imitate him. This irks Rishabh as he feels that in this entire exercise, he loses his dignity and respect in the eyes of Rishabh and his friends.

This is the Bhanot family:

Rishabh – 18-years old (college student)
Krishan Bhanot – Rishabh's father (in a private job)
Sushma Bhanot – Rishabh's mother (a beautician)
Ramit – Rishabh's younger brother

THE CONFLICT!!!

Rishabh's Diary

Sunday, March 25, nightfall

Today a picnic had been organised by papa's office. We were all very excited. Our family and families of some of papa's colleagues decided to go together, so we hired a small bus.

As usual papa came to my room and took one of my colourful tees. I could not refuse as I was already dressed so there was no question of my wearing it. I wanted to stop papa desperately, but knew better of it. As I had feared, everyone teased papa on the way, but he did not seem to mind. He was rather enjoying himself. I kept to myself.

I have learnt from my bad experiences. Papa loves dressing in my clothes since I became his size. Initially, I took pride in it thinking that papa approves of my choice. But when it became a routine, then it started getting on my nerves.

Whenever we would go for an outing, papa would scour through my almirah and fish out some trendy clothes which he dons shamelessly. He does not even care for that paunch which shows clearly through such clothes. He looks atrocious, but how to tell him this.

At times I tried to caution him indirectly, but he would pay no heed. Then I talked to mom about it, but she refused to interfere, knowing papa's hyperactive temper.

Many a time, I have seen his colleagues or friends sneering at him from behind at his weird sense of dressing. And to be fair to them, none of them ever wore such clothes. Papa would always look out of place in such gatherings. But that is for everyone else's eyes. To his eyes, he is the most chic, suave, modern person in that event.

Earlier, once before a picnic, I put all my tees for washing knowing fully well that he would again ask for one. But he threw such a tantrum that I swore to never do such a thing.

Today also he took out my maroon tee with dragon markings on it. He wore it with his new jeans (that he cannot borrow from me because our waists do not match) and was humming Justin Beiber while tying his laces.

Mom sniggers and Ramit seems amused, but no one says anything but it infuriates me to see my father making a fool of himself in front of everyone. He behaves as if he is a teenager in those clothes and I know everyone laughs at his expense.

I wonder when and how he will learn that age demands dignity. One should age with grace. Looking your age is beautiful – if only he could understand this fact of life.

I would like to ask him:

1. If he wants to wear such clothes, why does he not buy some for himself?

2. Does he never feel out of place when no one else wears these kinds of clothes?

3. Why doesn't mom put some wisdom in papa's head?

Rishabh

Counsellor Speaks

Some people do suffer from a kind of complex as they grow old and find their youth slipping away. The love of their family and trust of the family members in them helps them overcome this complex.

For Parents

- As a mother, it is your duty to see that your son does not harbour any ill feeling towards his father. Make him aware of the situation and not to criticise his father.
- If your son does not get to wear his favourite clothes because his father has borrowed them from him, then make sure he has some other alternate so that he does not feel deprived.

PARENTING Tip

Middle-age crisis is a passing phase. A teenager may not be able to relate to it because of the difference in age and thinking process.

Career Kit

In today's competitive world, it is a common norm to be ambitious. It is alright if the ambition is towards our own career and life. But when these ambitions cross the line and start influencing the lives of our children, then the trouble brews.

Raman and his family live in Amritsar. Raman's sister did her XII with PCB (physics, chemistry, biology) on the insistence of their father who wanted to be a doctor but could not become one. Unfortunately, Raman's sister could not clear any medical entrance tests and had to satisfy herself with simple bachelor's degree in science. Her dreams of becoming a computer engineer were drowned in her father's ambitions.

Let's meet Raman and his family:

Raman— 16 years old student (just passed X)
Jagdish Malhotra — Raman's father (bank employee)
Suman — Raman's mother (housewife)
Sanjana — Raman's 21-year-old sister (doing B.Sc.)

THE CONFLICT!!!

Raman's Diary

Friday, December 15, evening

They say history repeats itself and this is what is happening in our house. We all know that it was papa's biggest ambition to become a doctor. He could not fulfil it, so he has placed the burden of his ambition on our shoulders. Sanjana didi was his first victim. I still remember when didi had to choose her subjects in class XI, papa forced her to take biology instead of mathematics. Didi wanted to be an engineer, but daddy forced her to become a doctor and take biology instead. When she countered that she would take maths as the fifth subject, papa point-blankly refused saying that she will not be able to concentrate on her PCB subjects. Poor didi, she had no interest in biology still she was forced to study it. Besides that she had to take coaching for medical entrance exams. But what was the end result! She did not score well in XII boards because of excess work pressure. She did not get into any of the medical entrance exams because she had no interest in the subject. Ultimately, she had to do simple B.Sc. which never featured in her list of ambitions. Papa's ambitions shadowed her own ambitions. Today, she is a frustrated person who gets provoked very easily. She has no peace of mind and is no more a good student that she used to be earlier. On top of that, papa does not give up a single opportunity to remind her about the expenses he incurred due to her failed studies.

This year the same thing happened with me as I entered class XI. Now papa's focus has been shifted to me. I wanted to do law but he forced me to take the same science subjects as didi. I did not have the courage to go against his wishes. So I accepted it as my fate. But the results of my half-yearly exams showed how wrong I was. I failed in all the three core subjects, i.e. physics, chemistry and biology.

Today my class teacher called my father to school and advised him to change my stream. When I came home papa was in a bad mood.

He shouted at me for not concentrating on my studies. But I hope this scolding will bring something good for me. I wish he comes to his senses and allows me to take the subjects of my choice.

I wish I could ask him these questions-

1. Why does he force his ambitions on his children?

2. He has spoiled his daughter's career; still he has not woken up. Why does he want to repeat the same mistake with me?

3. Why does he keep reminding didi about the expenses he incurred on her coaching classes?

4. If his father was also like this, then he would have been ploughing the fields in the village and not working in the bank. Then why is he so adamant?

Raman

Counsellor Speaks

Most of the parents feel that their children are incapable of taking the right decisions about their career, so they try to guide their children. But somewhere along the way, this guidance turns into a command and children begin to feel pressurised under it. To be a true guide for your child, it is important that you do not cross that thin line.

For Parents

- You have good of your children in your heart, but your ideas do not match your children's ambitions. It is better to let the children follow their heart. Be supportive in their decisions and lend them financial and emotional support in what they want to do. Putting conditions like – you do what I want you to do then only I will pay for your fees – are not correct. The love and care of parents should be unconditional.

- You must remember one thing – every person is different. The ambitions and aptitude of your children is different from yours. So it is not justified that you force your ambitions on your children. Instead of telling them what they should do, be their friend and ask them lovingly as to what they want to do. This way you will nurture a good relationship with your children. At the same time, your children will be much happier if they are able to pursue their own choice of career.

- Money matters should never hamper the relationships. It is not right to remind children as to how much money has been spent on their education. It is the duty of the parents to provide for the children, so you should not boast about it and play these matters down.

Parenting Tip
It is good to be career-oriented, but to pass on your own ambitions to your children and then expecting them to fulfil those ambitions is not correct.

16

Playing Favourites

In our patriarchal society, the birth of a son is celebrated, while the birth of a daughter is condemned. This discrimination starts from the time of birth and goes on all throughout the life.

Let's meet Arya and her family. Arya lives in Kolkata with her family. Arya studies in a government school, while her younger brother studies in an expensive public school. Arya is good at studies and gets a merit scholarship from her school, still she is not given as many facilities, love and care in her house as her brother is given. Why? Let's read on.

This is the Sarkar-family:

Arya – 14 years old (class IX student of a government school)
Vimla – Arya's mother (housewife)
Vijay Sarkar – Arya's father, (a fourth division government employee)
Siddharth – Arya's 19-year-old brother (class XI student of a public school)

THE CONFLICT!!!

Arya's Diary

Monday, May 20, evening

Today I felt so alone. I went to the balcony and cried my heart out. What brought these tears was my result. I stood first in my class. Anyone would have been on the ninth cloud on getting such a result, and so was I. I came home so happy expecting ma and baba to praise me, but they were rather upset about Siddharth da failing in his class XI exam.

It hurts me so much. There is so much discrimination in this house. My brother gets all the good things in life. He goes to an English speaking public school, while I go to a government school. He repeated class X and now he has failed again in class XI, but the blame is put on his teachers for not training him properly. He takes tuitions for three subjects, while I have always studied on my own. He eats the best food, he gets the best clothes to wear. He even gets a pocket money every month. And what do I get – scoldings, sneers and a second grade treatment in my own house. I get praised for my efforts in my school and among my friends, but my own family spurns me just because I am a girl and Siddharth da is a boy.

There is never enough money in the house for me, but whenever Siddharth da needs something, he gets it. The other day, I told ma that I needed a pair of shoes badly as my shoes were completely torn. She told me to somehow manage for a week till baba got his salary. I agreed. But it hurts me when I found that baba had bought a new pair of sports shoes for Siddharth da for the practice of his school's sports day which was to be held next month. For him, Siddharth da's urgency was far greater than mine. That day I cried before my best friend and told her all about this discrimination. But she was helpless. What could she do?

I would like to ask my parents these things-

1. *Am I not their own daughter?*

2. *Why do they discriminate between their only son and daughter?*

3. *Why is it that Siddharth da's wish is their command, but for me they have no feelings?*

4. *Siddharth da could buy the new pair of shoes for his sports day later because it was to be held next month, but my shoes were completely torn. Whose urgency was more?*

Arya

Counsellor Speaks

Today girls are equal to boys in every field. So it is important that the parents treat them likewise and give them similar love and affection.

For Parents

- You should understand that in today's time, girls and boys are alike. It is wrong to discriminate between them. If you look around, you will find that many more girls look after their parents in their old age than boys do. As the government gives equal rights to both girls and boys, similarly, as a family you should grant equal love, affection, care and support to them.
- Your excessive love may spoil your son and your very little love may alienate your daughter from you. So balance your love for both of your children so that they both grow up to be good human beings.

PARENTING Tip

Discrimination between a girl and a boy is not a right thing. Even our country's law grants them equal rights, then who are we to create a division among them on the basis of gender?

The Locked Gate

If we rewind for a few years from now, discussing evil was not necessary with our children. Today the time has changed and so has the mindset. With crime rates so high, it is important to equip our children with knowledge of small time evils lurking around us.

Let's meet Suramya who lives in Bareilly with her mother and younger sister. Suramya lost her father three years ago. Her mother got a job in place of her father who was in a government job. As a single mother, it was a big responsibility for her to look after the finances to run the house, provide emotional support to her daughters and arrange for their security at home while she was away at work.

Let's meet Suramya's family:

Suramya – 17 years old (class XI student)
Shalini Bhatnagar – Suramya's mother (government employee)
Sairandhri – 13 years old (class VIII student)

THE CONFLICT!!!

Suramya's Diary

Tuesday, May 30, nightfall

Mummy is sleeping. I wanted to talk to her, but she was looking so tired that I did not say anything. I understand that she has so much work. She completes the housework before going to office. Although I help her by packing our tiffins, making beds and doing other sundry jobs, but still she does most of the work. Then the whole day she is in the office. In the evening, she buys provisions before coming home. Then she cooks dinner and we eat. Sometimes, when I have some problem, she helps me with my homework. I try not to bother her with other problems. But at times, I wish papa was alive and she could be at home all the time with us so that we could share all our problems with her.

This Sunday also I tried to talk to her about Sujit uncle. He is papa's friend. He sometimes comes over and help us in things like depositing bills, some minor repairs in the house and even in our studies. He is married but has no children, so I presumed that he showers his love on us. But last week, this delusion was broken. Sujit uncle came to our house. Sairandhri and I had just come back from school. Uncle sat down with us and chatted for a while. Then I excused myself and went inside to change my dress. Sairandhri remained with uncle telling him all about her school. She loves to talk, especially about her friends. After changing my clothes as I was coming into the drawing room, I saw uncle standing behind Sairandhri rubbing her back. His one hand was slowly slipping towards the front of her dress. I was shocked to see all this. As usual, Sairandhri was unaware of all of this. She was busy narrating her day's events. I entered the room making a lot of noise. Uncle immediately pulled his hands back and left almost immediately on the pretext of some important work. I did not know what to say to Sairandhri so I decided to tell mummy all this. May be she could tell Sujit uncle not to come here in her absence and counsel

Sairandhri to be careful. On Sunday, I broached the subject and told her about the entire incident. To my dismay, mummy did not attach much importance to this episode. She just nodded and told me to be around and not leave Sairandhri alone with anyone. I asked her if she would admonish Sujit uncle for this, she just nodded absentmindedly and left the room. I wish dadi would come soon and stay with us forever. But whenever she comes, it is only for a short while and even during that time, she and mummy continue to fight with each other.

I wish mummy would devote more time to us. My friends tell me how their mothers discuss their problems and find solutions for them. They know all about sex education, abuses and many other things which I am totally unaware of. In fact, more than my mother, it is my friends with whom I feel comfortable discussing my problems. At least, they listen to me patiently and give me a solution.

I wish I could ask my mother these things –

1. She claims that she is doing everything for her daughters, then why can't she take out even a few minutes to talk to us when we need her?

2. Why does she not tell us about sex and other such taboo subjects about which we cannot discuss with outsiders?

3. Why do we need help from such a lecherous person like Sujit uncle?

4. Why can't dadi come and live with us forever?

Suramya

Counsellor Speaks

Adolescence is such a delicate stage of life when you are neither an adult nor a child. Care, love and attention bestowed by the parents to their adolescent children can help them face tricky situations of this stage.

For Parents

- As a mother it is your duty to not only provide your children with necessities of life, but to solve their problems however big or small they may be.
- Remember, it is only for a few more years that they are going to be with you. This is the time when they are the most vulnerable and anything gone wrong with their life during this period may cause havoc for them forever. So do not ignore when your daughter complain of Sujit's overtures and try to solve it in the best possible manner.
- You cannot be with your daughters all the time, but you can provide them with such emotional security that they feel your presence even when you are not there. For this, you need to take time out from your busy schedule. If not on weekdays, then at least on weekends, you should find time to talk to your daughters.

Parenting Tip

Your children need you beside them more than anything else. As a parent, it is your duty to give them the time and attention they rightly deserve from you.

18

Boiling Over...

Anxiety is not good for anyone. It brings on anger and then we tend to say or do things irrationally.

Let's meet Rahul who lives in Gurgaon. His father is a businessman and quite short-tempered. In his anger, he tends to over-react over things which are otherwise mundane.

> **This is Rahul's family:**
>
> Rahul – 17 years old (student of class XI)
> Rima – Rahul's mother (housewife)
> Tarun Khandelwal – Rahul's father (businessman)
> Simran – Rahul's 12-year-old sister

THE CONFLICT!!!

Rahul's Diary

Sunday, November 19, nightfall

What could have been a fun day today turned into a terrible day – thanks to my father. I had made some great plans along with my friend for today, as we decided to go to IITF (India International Trade Fair) at Pragati Maidan in the morning. There were about ten of us, six guys and four girls. We had planned to start early in the metro so that we could get entry on time. All was set. Everyone had taken permission from their parents. I asked mummy and she had no objections. I had even taken out the clothes which I would wear in the morning. I was glad papa was not in town, otherwise he would again have got hyper and denied me permission to go with my friends. He was to return from his business tour on Monday morning, by then I would be back home and he would not even get to know what had transpired behind his back.

In the morning as I was getting ready, I heard the doorbell, thinking them to be my friends, I rushed to open the door and there stood my father and the doom of my plans for IITF. Sure enough, seeing me ready so early in the morning, he asked me. I had no choice but to reply. And as expected, he got hyper and released so much steam that I was forced to call off my plans to IITF. I complied and then went into my room sulking the whole day. I could hear mummy trying to make him see reason, but he was adamant. 'He is not old enough... what if there is an accident... what if he is not able to find his way back home... what if something happened at the fair... it is a Sunday and on a holiday, this fair is so crowded. Suppose a bomb went off there ..., I wish it does here so, I am saved from this prison.'

This is not the first time that he has behaved like this. He has this tendency of getting hyper over little things. I remember when I got a D grade in my maths paper last year, he raved and ranted for almost an hour with all his possible what's and if's. "What if he failed next year... what if he is denied permission to opt for maths in class XI.." My god, father give me a break. Class XI was so far away still he could foresee things. I wonder, if this is what is known as being farsighted!

I know mummy tries to take my side, but she is subdued by my father. If given a chance, I would like to ask my parents these questions –

1. Why does he always imagine bad things?

2. What makes him think that his predictions for the future will always hold true?

3. Who is he to take all the decisions of my life?

4. Why is he always so negative in his thinking and deeds?

Rahul

Counsellor Speaks

We all have our shares of good and bad memories. But they should remain only in the past and not influence our present. If they start hampering our and others' life, then they best be forgotten.

For Parents

- ❐ Rahul's father needs psychiatric help. In fact, he should have sought it long ago. However, it is never too late. You should take him to a good psychiatrist and have him remove the fear, bad memories and insecurities from his psyche.

- ❐ Rahul is at such a tender age that these confrontations with his father may wound his heart forever. So be gentle to him and try to make him understand the situation from another perspective. You can even act as a bridge between the father and the son.

- ❐ You may even try to make your husband understand that Rahul is not a child anymore and it is his right to a certain freedom in life. Ask him to place himself in Rahul's place and then see his reaction. You may even rope in your mother-in-law to help you control the situation.

PARENTING Tip

We should nurture our children like blooming flowers. Treating them harshly may lead to their withering.

19

Nag...Nag...Nag...

Sometimes in our haste to complete work, we tend to push others. This may be acceptable once in a while, but when it stretches to days on end, then it turns into nagging.

Anupama lives in Pune. Her mother is a housewife and obsessed with perfection. Anupama is a well-behaved and diligent child, but sometimes, she gets upset when nagging in the house goes overboard.

Let's meet Anupama and her family:

Anupama – 15 years old (Class IX student)
Anuradha – Anupama's mother (housewife)
Devender Vyas – Anupama's father (accountant)
Avnindra – Anupama's 11-year-old brother

THE CONFLICT!!!

Anupama's Diary

Sunday, January 16, afternoon

After an entire morning of nagging, I could finally escape to my room. Being a Sunday, everyone was at home and thus, began the nagging around in the house from early in the morning. First it was household chores, then studies and later cleaning of my room.

I quietly complied and completed every task she gave me. Then I sat down to study when she insisted. By noon, I was tired and wanted something to eat. But what I got was just a banana and two oranges. Why wasn't the food ready, I would like to ask, but dare not. I suppose she was too busy nagging all of us that she could not prepare food on time. Then she came to my room and started off as to how dirty my room was. That was the last straw. I just blew my head off and there it was – another blasted Sunday added to the list of the doomed Sundays in my memory.

But this is so frustrating.

I don't know why she nags so much. She has to find fault with everything. Even if the room is clean, she will find a speck of dust somewhere and would go on and on forever.

If one of the dishes she is cooking does not turn out to her satisfaction, she would get into a bad mood and take out her anger on us.

She would nag us for delay in bath... for not making bed properly... for not keeping things in place... and so many more such things... the list is endless.

She nags daddy for not giving her the best of all comforts that her kitty party friends have.

She nags Avnindra for not being such a scholar as our neighbour's son who studies with him in his class.

Nagging has become a way of life for her. She always has a frown on her face.

I don't remember ever seeing her happy in the house. The only time she has a smile on her face is when her kitty party friends come over. Even that smile seems pasted.

I wish I could ask her these things:

1. *Why does she keep searching for perfection in us?*

2. *Has she ever looked at herself? Is she as perfect as she expects us to be?*

3. *Doesn't she ever realise that her nagging seems to take us far away from her?*

4. *Why can't she lead a normal life like other mothers and be loving and forgiving to us?*

Anupama

Counsellor Speaks

Discipline and perfection are important in life, but not to the extent that they start hampering the relationships. Be flexible in your approach and make your home environment comfortable and relaxed and not just plastic perfect.

For Parents
- You may have good reasons for pushing children in doing various jobs, but if it goes beyond its limit then it gets irritating. So do not nag them.
- Sunday is a day for relaxation for the whole family. Do not expect them to overwork themselves when they are in holiday mood. In fact, if you want a perfect Sunday then do not insist on getting all the work done first and then sit down to relax. For you, a clean home, sparkling kitchen etc may be a priority, but it may not be so with others. Sunday is equally precious for them as they too would like to unwind and rest. So do your cleaning, etc., done on Saturdays and leave the Sundays for only relaxation. In fact, you should also relax so that you are ready to face another week rejuvenated.

PARENTING Tip
Don't let nagging become a habit with you. Just put yourself in the shoes of those whom you nag. This will help you realise how irritating it is.

Food Row

Eating fast food has become a norm of today. Teenagers adopt it more as a fad. This may sometimes lead to difference of opinion between the parents and the teenagers.

Let's meet Supreet who belongs to a middle class family. They hail from interiors of Punjab and now live in Delhi. His father established his business in Delhi and shifted his family here.

This is Supreet's family:

Supreet – 19 years old (college student)
Pinky – Supreet's mother (housewife)
Gurusharan Singh – Supreet's father (businessman)
Sweety – Supreet's 16-year-old sister

THE CONFLICT!!!

Supreet's Diary

Saturday, August 15, nightfall

There was such a big row in the house over food today that I now feel like going away from this place somewhere far away. This is how it started.

Food is one topic in our household which is discussed in detail. Papa insists that we should eat clean, home cooked food. Mummy is always trying out new recipes and forcing them down our throats. Sweety is almost always on diet, so it suits her to eat home-cooked food which in any case she eats so little. But I love to eat out, especially at fast food joints. They are good places for hang out. You go with friends and spend hours there without ever feeling out of place. Even the food there is much more interesting than what we get at home. Almost every other day, I eat there with my friends. Sometimes, papa gets to know and then he cribs. So most of the times, I try to hide the fact and eat little food at home. Mummy would always crib that I have started eating very little food just like Sweety but I would laugh it off.

Last night, as I put my jeans for washing, I forgot to empty my pockets. They were full of bills of fast food joints. It seems when mummy was emptying out the pockets, papa was at home as his office was closed due to Independence Day. He saw the bills. It didn't take them long to put two and two together.

He didn't even wait for me to wake up. He first shouted for me then he shouted at me.

The day was such a nightmare that I do not ever want to relive it. I wish I could make them understand that more than half of my generation sustains on fast food. And I do not see any problem in them or their health. I don't know why they always insist upon eating only good home-cooked food and always criticise the fast food by calling it junk food.

I wish I could ask my parents these questions:

1. Food is food, then why discriminate between them as good and bad foods?

2. When everyone eats fast foods, why am I stopped from eating out?

3. I do like mom's cooking and appreciate it too, but why force it down my throat all the time?

4. Why make such an issue if I eat out once in a while?

Supreet

Counsellor Speaks

There are various stages in the life of a teenager which pass away with time. Worrying excessively about them only brings stress to both the sides.

For Parents

- Peer pressure affects teenagers badly. So do not be angry with Supreet for giving in to the peer pressure. Do not scold him and try to make him see reason lovingly.
- Inculcate the confidence in Supreet that you will not scold him even if he eats out. Also you should not force him to eat at home on a full stomach. This way, at least he will not eat excess food and put on weight.
- Divert Supreet's attention to some healthy habits like going to gym or playing an outdoor sport. This way he will remain fit and learn to eat healthy foods.

Parenting Tip

Junk food is not good for health, but eating any food in excess is equally bad.

21

Exam Stress

Exams form an integral part of the adolescence. Teenagers spend the best part of their life in school busy with their studies and exams.

Let us meet Garvi who lives in Gorakhpur. She lives with her parents, who have great dreams for her future.

This is Garvi's family:

Garvi – 17 years old (student of class XII)
Ayushi – Garvi's mother (housewife)
Dharmendra Vyas – Garvi's father (an engineer)
Arushi – Garvi's elder sister doing third year B.Sc.

THE CONFLICT!!!

Garvi's Diary

Thursday, April 13, night

My first engineering entrance exam is three days away. As soon as my XII board exams finished, mom made my life miserable. She had filled up various forms of different engineering colleges. She even brought me many books for entrance exams and warned me that I must finish each one of them before entrance exams. She even gave me the exact amount of money she spent on them making me feel all the more guilty.

Instead of allowing me to take rest for a day or two, she pushed me headlong in another whirlpool of studies.

She even got me to join the crash course which started almost soon after my board exams.

I felt helpless and very tired all the time, but could not say anything.

But today, mummy crossed the limit. Sharma uncle and aunty, our family friends, had come over for lunch. Their daughter Supriya, who is a little younger than me, had also come. She is in class XI. I thought I would also go out of my room and have lunch with everyone and then go back to my room. After lunch, the group of elderly went to the balcony for coffee. Mummy instructed me to go inside and study, while Arushi didi could accompany Supriya. They were watching a comedy movie. It was very interesting. I also sat down with them and somehow got so engrossed in it that I did not see the time. When mummy came inside to call Supriya, as her parents were leaving, she was enraged to see me sitting in front of TV. At that time, she did not say anything. As soon as the Sharmas departed, she came inside huffing and puffing and put the TV off. She then started yelling on top of her voice. When Arushi didi tried to pacify her, she brushed her aside and took her to task too. I was already peeved on getting such a harsh scolding for simply watching bit of a movie for half an hour and on top of that when she started accusing Arushi didi for not only ignoring her own studies – she had given entrances for pre-medical, but could not clear any even after two attempts – but also putting her influence on me. In her anger, mummy ignored the fact that it was her own daughters that she was cursing. I could not bear this and told her not to make Arushi didi a scapegoat. At this Arushi didi started crying and even though I felt the same, my anger took the better of me.

I could have had a row with her, but just then papa came inside. Arushi didi ran into her room and I to mine. Papa is a heart patient, so we avoid any sort of conflict before him. His presence even shut down mummy and all was quiet for a while.

But I would like to ask her these questions:

1. Why does she pressurise me so much for studies? I also know what is good for me.

2. No one can study twenty-four hours in a day. Why does she not understand this?

3. Why does she blame Arushi didi for my failures as well as her own failures? Why does she treat her as a scapegoat?

4. If she has bought me so many competition books, does this mean that I am obliged to study them all? The forced manner in which I am asked to study makes me want to rebel.

Garvi

Counsellor Speaks

In today's competitive world, studying more is never enough. While children need to understand the extent of this competition, parents must also understand that putting extra stress on the children cannot get better results. So it is important to keep their cool and allow the children to be cool too.

For Parents

- ☐ You are ambitious, but that does not mean that your daughter may be equally ambitious. Do not force yourself on your children and let them study on their own pace.
- ☐ Even if Garvi does not clear this year's entrance exam, there is still next year when she can study hard and get good grades.
- ☐ Do not compare your two daughters with each other and do not degrade any one before the other. Remember every person is different in their own way.
- ☐ Neither take nor give stress to your daughter just before the exams. She has been passing her exams till now and will do so in future. Have faith in her abilities.

Parenting Tip

A little stress is good for us as it provides us reason enough to move ahead in life, but excess of stress may be distressing and we may lose our confidence because of it.

It's So Crowded

With changing times, the family system has also been changing. Earlier most of the people lived in joint families, but now the trend has shifted to nuclear families. Whether it is because of migration from rural to urban areas or because of western influence, is difficult to say.

Let's meet Garima who lives in Mumbai. Earlier, she lived with her parents as a nuclear family. Recently, her grandfather died in Patiala and her grandmother had to come to Mumbai to live with them along with her youngest unmarried daughter. Garima finds her small flat very crowded these days.

Let's meet Garima and her family:

Garima – 14 years old (studies in class VIII)
Sangita – Garima's mother (housewife)
Ashok Sahni – Garima's father (employed in a private firm as clerk)
Sanchit – Garima's 11-year-old brother (studies in class V)
Dayawati Sahni – Garima's grandmother
Shalini – Garima's aunt (yet to be married)

THE CONFLICT!!!

Garima's Diary

Saturday, June 20, midnight

Oh, this is getting so irritating. Today, I was watching my favourite Hollywood movie on TV when suddenly Dadi (grandmother) appeared from nowhere and changed the channel to some silly Punjabi movie. I protested that I was watching my movie, but she told me off saying that I watch my English movies all the time, but this Punjabi movie will not be aired on TV again. I was about to retaliate when Bua (father's sister) also came and sat with Dadi and they both soon got engrossed in the movie. I went to ma (mother), but she could only sympathise with me which did not really help.

Since Dadi and Bua shifted here from Patiala, the house has become so crowded and different. It does not seem like my home. Everything is done according to their whims and fancies. She does not eat non-vegetarian food, so we have also stopped eating it. She does not like my going to parties or to my friends' house, so papa has posed a restriction on my going out alone. I do manage somehow with ma in on my secret, is another matter.

Even the house seems so crowded. There are only two bedrooms in our house. One is of ma and papa's and the other one which was mine and Sanchit's has been given to Dadi and Bua. Now all our things are scattered here and there. We sleep in the hall, we study in ma's room and our cupboard with clothes and other things is lying in the store. Sometimes, we cannot even sleep properly when Dadi watches TV till late at night because the TV is kept in the hall.

I have stopped calling my friends over. It's been a long time since we had a party at home or even went for an outing. It seems this is how our life is going to be forever, because Dadi and Bua have come here for good.

I wish there was a solution to my problem. I want to ask my parents these things :

1. *Why can't we go back to our earlier way of life?*

2. *If we can't, then why can't we move into a bigger house so that everyone can live properly?*

3. *Even if Dadi is living here, why must she interfere in our lives?*

4. *If nothing can be done, please ma, papa, send me to a hostel. I don't like it here at all. Can you do that?*

Garima

Counsellor Speaks

After living in a nuclear family for so many years, it becomes difficult to adjust in a joint family. While nuclear family comes with a certain freedom, joint family poses many bonds which seem too binding if relations are not congenial.

For Parents

- It seems that there is some discord between the family members because of change in lifestyle. You may have a heart-to-heart talk with everyone and settle the matters before they go out of hand.
- If it is possible financially to take a bigger house, then all matters could be solved. May be if your mother pitches in some money, if she is financially secure, then your lifestyle would be much better and everyone will live in peace.
- It is important for children to concentrate on their studies. If possible, get a small TV set for your mother and sister and install it in their room so that children are not disturbed during studies and they can sleep on time at night.

Parenting Tip

Life holds many surprises for us. It is for us to decide how we react to them.

I Am Not Yours

The bond between a child and the parents is special. No one can break that bond. This bond has its roots in the love and affection that both feel for each other.

Does being an adopted child or a biological child have any affects on this bond? Let's meet Mita who is an adopted child. Her parents legally adopted her from an orphanage after ten years of their marriage and showered all their love and affection on her. Being liberal and open-minded, they did not hide this fact from her and on her 18th birthday told her everything. Should Mita feel angry, hurt or obliged?

This is Mita's family:

Mita – 18 years old (studies in class XII)
Manju – Mita's mother (housewife)
Mahendra Nath – Mita's father (businessman)

THE CONFLICT!!!

Mita's Diary

Tuesday, July 15, midnight

Today is my birthday and today my world turned upside down. I turned eighteen today, and we had a big party in the house. I had invited all my friends. There was a huge two-tier cake and we all had so much fun like every year. But it all lasted till the end of the party. After seeing the last guest, mom and dad called me into the study and asked me to sit down. They said that they wanted to tell me something. I was tired but the day's excitement had still not worn off. I was sure, dad would give me another surprise like a proposal to go to UK to study after XII as I had been after his life to get me admission through his contacts there.

But what I heard was more of a jolt than pleasant news. In a matter of fact way, they told me that I was not their daughter by birth. I was their adopted daughter. Although they loved me from the bottom of their heart, but this was the truth according to them, I should be aware of.

Seeing me in a state of shock, mom hugged me and reassured me that nothing would change. They were telling me the truth so that later I did not feel cheated. How could I tell her that I was already feeling cheated?

I came into my room and sobbed till the tears could flow no more. Unsettled in my mind, I could recall many incidents when people threw hints, but I never took. Like when we went to Singapore, one of dad's friends commented that I did not look like any of my parents. I never took him seriously then, but today his words are pinching me.

Even my father's mother, it seems, has never approved of my adoption. She would always coax my mother to try for another child which ma would just smile and ignore. Dadi never picked me in her lap, nor did she ever give me her blessing. Earlier, I used to think that being an orthodox person; she wanted a grandson, that is why she disliked me as a girl was born in her family. But today, I know the true reason behind that hatred and I can totally justify her for not being able to accept someone else's child as her own granddaughter.

Today I would like to ask my parents these questions:

1. Why did they not tell me of this truth earlier? I feel like such a fool for being in dark for so long.

2. For that matter, why did they tell me this truth at all? If they could hide it for 18 years, they could have done so for a few more years, may be, till I became more mature.

3. Who were my biological parents? Can I go searching for them?

4. What would be my status in this house after revelation of this truth to me?

Mita

Counsellor Speaks

Adolescence is a stage when you are neither a child nor an adult. You are not expected to act childish and at the same time, you cannot act mature either.

For Parents

- ☐ You did the right thing in waiting for Mita to grow up before telling her the truth. Although she may take some time to digest this news, but soon she will become normal.
- ☐ Now that the truth is out and there are no more skeletons in the closet, just bury everything at the back of the mind and never ever again take up this subject. Even if Mita tries to talk about it, stop her firmly then and there. This was an information that you wanted to give to her and not a future plan that you ought to discuss time and again.
- ☐ Indulge Mita in studies and other activities. Be loving and caring to her as earlier. Do not let her feel as if something is amiss which actually is not. If she ever asks to go in pursuit of her biological parents, be firm and tell her not to chase after unknown. She is your daughter and she will understand your concern.

PARENTING Tip

Caring for an adopted child should neither be treated as a favour to the child, nor a noble deed, or a charity. It is the pure love of a parent. Do not disgrace this love by finding any selfish motive in it.

24

Special Needs

It is a misconception that we should treat children with special needs differently. If you ask them you would understand that they too like to be treated as normal.

Let's meet Robin who is hearing impaired. Robin lives in Goa. He has a loving family, but sometimes, he likes to be independent because he feels that he can look after himself.

This is Robin's family:

Robin – 16 years old (studies in class X)
Mary – Robin's mother (housewife)
Joseph Fernandez – Robin's father (shopowner)
Rubaina – Robin's sister (studies in second year college)

THE CONFLICT!!!

Robin's Diary

Sunday, December 23, evening

Today was the day when I sang my first carol before the church audience. It was not solo, I was in a group, but it was a good feeling. Till a year ago, I had never thought I would be able to sing. But the speech therapy I received was amazing. Now I can speak despite my inability to hear.

But my family still thinks otherwise. Papa never believed that I could achieve such a feat. So when I told them in the morning that I would be singing at the church, they seemed unmoved. I would have expected some excitement from them because after all, I had planned it as a surprise, but there was no response from any of them. It was a great opportunity to be able to sing on this Sunday, but they had other things to worry. There were numerous questions in their minds like if I missed a beat, if I went out of tune and never got to know of it because I cannot hear the music and so on. Thank God! I could not hear their concern. I could lip read, but I decided to avert my eyes and set off to the church determinedly. Their apprehensions were justified, but at least, they should have shown some faith in me.

Everything went well and I did not do anything wrong. I expected mom and papa to be happy, but instead they looked so tense. While coming back as I was trying to cross the road, mom tried to take my hand so that I could cross the road safely. Now I am not a child. So I refused to do so. But then she got angry and forced me to take her hand. I did not like it but instead of making a scene on the road, I decided to tow the line.

When dad unlocked the car, I was the first to get in. I waited for sometime, but no one came in, I looked out and saw some of our relatives standing outside congratulating mom and papa. On seeing me, they rushed towards me and hugged me. I was happy and I thanked them with my new found speech. But at the same time, it hurts me that mom and papa did not call me out to meet them when they had come to congratulate me.

I would like to ask these things from my parents –

1. Are they ashamed to have me as their son?

2. Why do they try to overprotect me? Would they have done the same even if they had a normal son?

3. Why do they want to be my ears when I can very well read the lip movement?

4. When will they understand that I need their love not help?

Robin

Counsellor Speaks

Life for a challenged child may seem difficult for us, but it is not always so. God gives his people enough courage to overcome any crisis. So what seems like a handicap to you, may be just a way of life for that person who is born with it. So do not judge others with your own perception. Give your child his independence to follow his dreams.

For Parents

- You must understand that being a hearing impaired child, it is not easy for Robin to accept this fact that he is in some way less than anyone else. He wants to live a normal life and is making efforts in that direction. Your being overprotective may hurt his pride. So be a little tactful.
- Treat him like a normal person and share his joys and sorrows as equals. Do not hide things from him. Open communication channels with him. He may be slow to grasp initially, but soon you both will understand each other well.
- Do not try to help him when not required. Just instill this confidence in him that help is just a call away for him. Do not try to jump in every situation that he can handle on his own.

Parenting Tip

God helps those who help themselves. Make your child independent and not dependent on you.

Listen to Me

Some people show attention-seeking behaviour. This may stem from some childhood experiences, low esteem or inferiority complex.

Abhishek lives in Jaipur. He is the youngest son of his parents. His eldest brother Abhinav is bright in studies, while the second brother Anuj is a good sportsperson. Abhishek is a mediocre in every field. He is an average student and has no interest in sports. Since he feels inferior to his brothers, being the youngest in the family, he often throws tantrums.

Let's meet Abhishek and his family.

Abhishek – 14 years old (studies in class VIII)
Abhinav – 22 years old (doing MBA)
Anuj – 18 years old (plays cricket at national level)
Aradhana – Abhishek's mother (lecturer)
Dr. Vishwa Mohan Singh – Abhishek's father (Doctor)

THE CONFLICT!!!

Abhishek's Diary

Saturday, April 10, midnight

Why did God make me? I am so average in a household full of achievers.

Today Verma uncle and his wife came for dinner. He is a senior consultant in daddy's nursing home. It was a nice cool evening. After dinner, dad asked everyone to move to the balcony for coffee. Abhinav bhaiya (brother) and Anuj bhaiya were not at home, so I did not feel like sitting with elders and excused myself on the pretext of studying. I had not even reached my room when I heard Verma uncle talking to dad in hushed tones. The broken pieces of conversation that I could hear were enough for me to guess what or rather who was the topic of their conversation. They were discussing me. I stayed a little longer and did some eves dropping. Verma uncle was telling dad as to how I was a misfit in their family of geniuses. Dad was explaining how he has tried to give me the best of everything still I could not improve. Before they could discuss my incompetency in detail, I turned around and rushed to my room and shut the door with a bang. I wanted to throw my books on the floor and break the mirror like I did last week when Suman mausi (mother's sister) was counselling mom about how she should send me to a hostel to up my low self-esteem. On hearing the commotion, they had all come to my room and Suman mausi called my anger as attention seeking behaviour. Mom was so angry that she could have slapped me that day had dad not stopped her.

I don't know what happens to me sometimes. I do not like myself to be compared with my brothers or my parents who are all well established in their respective lives. Sometimes, I wonder if I am their own flesh and blood, or they have brought me from somewhere. I am so average in every field that I can't even in my wildest dreams think of accomplishing what my brothers have accomplished.

Dad is patient with me. He tries to pacify me, whenever I do something wild, but when Abhinav and Anuj bhaiya are around he adores them and not me.

I wish I could ask my parents these questions:

1. *Why does dad allow others to speak ill of me?*
2. *Is it my fault that I am such an average person? Why can't they accept me with all my faults?*
3. *Why do they keep on comparing me with my brothers?*
4. *Why can't I get the same love and attention that those two get?*

Abhishek

Counsellor Speaks

Many children show attention seeking behaviour when they are low on confidence. This habit should be curbed as soon as possible by dealing with the child in gentle, yet firm way.

For Parents

- You must give this confidence to Abhishek that you love him as much as you love his brothers. For this, you will have to be very patient.
- Do not reprimand him or beat him if he again tries any of his attention seeking tactics, instead be firm with him and tell him how you expect him to act maturely and not in this childish manner.
- Remember to neither criticise him before others, nor take criticism in his name from anyone else. Once he realises that you are on his side, he will come out of his shell quickly.

PARENTING Tip

Not every child is alike in a family. It is the role of the parents to deal with them in an appropriate manner.

Adolescence

Adolescence is a period of turbulent changes for the child, both mentally as well as physically. From a distance, they seem like wonder years because they hold so many facets of life in them. But these are also the years when one realises that the life is not just a bed of roses.

The Wonder Years

Every child steps into adolescence cherishing great hopes of the adult world. The transition is also welcomed because it seems to offer an end to parental dependence. At this stage, it seems that there would be no problems and it would be an easy task to pursue one's goals in life. The adolescence not only ushers greater hopes of adult life but also the new trials and tribulations as tag alongs.

A closer look reveals that adult life is not as attractive as it appeared to be from a distance. However the picture is not so gloomy after all. All it needs is a cool attitude towards life. The adolescents need to listen, observe, evaluate and accept various aspects of life without mulling over them unnecessarily. They must learn to accept life as it is and not as they would like it to be.

Peer Pressure

Till adolescence, the family has the most important influence on the children. But now there is a drastic change. Parents are no longer the undisputed guides and the centre of their focus. The friends slowly take their place and begin to command their loyalty. Suddenly, it becomes very important for them to be appreciated and accepted by their peer group rather than by the family. Peer pressure can be negative or positive. It may range from academic achievement to smoking, etc. whichever way, being a member of a peer group means a lot more fun for the teenagers.

Family Support

Though peer group is very important for the teenagers, the support of the family is crucial for them. This lessens the teenagers' vulnerability to negative pressure from peers. Parents may act as role models and set standards for their teenage children by sharing a positive and warm relationship with them.

Media Influence

Media creates some brand icons in the form of celebrities from the fields of sport, entertainment or politics. Teenagers swear by these icons and like to imitate them in every respect. They also begin to act and behave like them without considering the inevitable difference. Every teenage boy dreams of looking like a hunky and athletic film star or a teenage girl wants to look like a tall, beautiful and slim model, but few can match their idols in real life. It is important for the teenagers to be practical and not get carried away by such influences. A good educational background and a gentle and tactful curtailment by parents can help ward off such media influence.

Grievances

Parents Talk

Q1. My son speaks rudely with us. Any type of cajoling or gentle talk does not seem to make him realise his folly. What should I do?

Ans. First of all, you must analyse your own behaviour and assess if you have ever been rude to him. Most of the times, children like to imitate their parents. They learn habits, good or bad, from their parents. Show him with your actions that you do not like this way of talking and he must amend his ways.

Q2. My daughter watches TV all the time even at the expense of her studies. Ours is a joint family, so the TV is always on in our house. What should I do?

Ans. Provide your daughter a room farthest to TV, where she can study in peace. Since you cannot stop others from watching TV, you will have to make your daughter understand the importance of studies. Allot her a specific time during which she should study. In rest of her free time, do not stop her from watching TV, if she wants.

Q3. Despite my repeated warnings, my 15-year-old son takes my bike and goes for a ride with his friends. I have a touring job so I am out of town most of the time. What should I do?

Ans. You have only two options – either you rein in your son or sell your bike. Because if your son is caught riding a bike without licence, he may be prosecuted. So take a firm stand. If you are not there, ask your wife to be firm and not hand over the keys of the bike to your son. Gently make him understand that he should wait for a few years till he gets his licence.

Q4. I am a morning person and I want my children to be up early. But they like to study till late at night and wake up late too. Am I wrong in teaching them some good habits?

Ans. You are absolutely right that waking up early in the morning keeps you fresh and healthy. If they are so adamant on studying at night, you may ask them to try this new schedule for a few days and see how different they feel and fare in studies. If your children still prefer night time to study than the morning hours then let them be.

Q5. ***Ours is a very religious family. We often have havans and kirtans in our house. My daughter who is in class XII gets very irritated because of this. Although we have given her a separate room for study, still she continues to complain as the hustle-bustle of the function disturbs her. What should I do?***

Ans. You may have made all the arrangements you deem fit for your daughter so that she won't get disturbed, but the problem is that she is still getting disturbed. You may try sending her to her friend's house or to a relative's house nearby, where she can study without interference.

Parenting Quiz

None of us is born a good parent. There are no set standards for parenting. It comes naturally to parents as they grow with their children. In some ways, our way of dealing with a child is reminiscent of our childhood experiences. Here is a quiz for all you parents. Below are listed a set of questions which would enable you to gauge yourself through your response to them. Answer these questions by marking the most appropriate choice given below each of them.

1. *After coming back from work when your son quite excitedly tries to tell you about his cricket match, do you*

    a) listen carefully.
    b) listen half-heartedly.
    c) ignore him and put on the TV instead.
    d) snub him and go inside to freshen up.

2. *You have told your son to unroll his socks after taking them off and putting for washing. If he does not do it even after your many reminders, you*

    a) wash only those socks that are unrolled.
    b) continue to unroll them yourself.
    c) complain to your husband.
    d) lose your temper and give him a good scolding.

3. *Your daughter knocked down a vase while cleaning the side table, you*

    a) ask her if she was hurt.
    b) give her a warning to be careful next time.
    c) make her clean the glass pieces as a punishment.
    d) tell her to replace the vase.

4. *Your son is going on a field trip from school for the first time, you*

    a) give him required instructions and tell him to have fun.
    b) become extremely hyper and write down a long 'to do' list for him.

c) give him unending advices.
   d) refuse to send him alone till they allow you to accompany him.

5. **Your daughter came two hours late from her friend's party, even her mobile phone was switched off, you**
   a) make her understand gently that this kind of behaviour is not acceptable from a responsible person.
   b) call up all her friends to find out her whereabouts.
   c) be firm with her and tell her that this kind of behaviour will not be tolerated the next time.
   d) have already been to the police station to lodge an FIR.

6. **Your son wants to go abroad to study, but you cannot afford it, you**
   a) advise him to look for option of scholarships and loans and promise to help him in availing them.
   b) take a heavy loan beyond your capacity so that your son can fulfil his most cherished dream.
   c) tell him that he cannot go because you do not have such funds.
   d) give him two tight slaps so that this stupid idea never again enters his mind.

7. **Your daughter tells you about a man who is stalking her to school, you**
   a) make sure that you daughter does not go to school alone till this problem is sorted out.
   b) complain to police and leave everything to them.
   c) confront that man and break his nose.
   d) take her out of the school and make her study from home.

8. **Your son had a difference of opinion with your father and a huge argument ensued, you would**
   a) make your son say sorry to his grandfather first before doing anything else.
   b) remain detached from the entire episode.
   c) sort out the problem by intervening between them.
   d) make your father say sorry to your son.

9. **Your 16-year old son wants to buy a motorbike, you would**
   a) make him understand that he cannot ride it before he is 18 years old.

b) give in to his demands but do not allow him to ride on the main road.
   c) tell him firmly that he must first get his driving licence made.
   d) buy him the bike and get him the driving licence by bribing the officials.

10. Your daughter is always talking to her friends on the mobile. You do not like it. You
   a) sit down with her and make her understand that life should be balanced between many activities.
   b) do not care because you also talk on the mobile most of the time.
   c) give her a warning that if she does not behave, you will confiscate her mobile.
   d) ban her from using the mobile at all.

Interpretation

In your answers to the above questions, in all probability, you have checked the same key-letter – a, b, c or d several times. if the same letter has been checked six to eight times, your parenting type is quite definite. If your selections are scattered, you may be a combination of any two of the following.

Read the analysis.

The A type

Your parenting style is gentle, yet firm. You know what is right for your child and deliver it to the child in the right manner. You do not nag and command a lot of respect from your children. They know that they can rely on you at all times.

The B type

You are mostly cool and relaxed to the extent that you seem damn care. You seem to be unaffected with things with a certain degree of lassitude in your life. Such people are not taken seriously by others. So stop being so lax and overly considerate. Learn to stress your point whenever needed.

The C type

You are generally understanding, but at times, you become impulsive and temperamental. Sometimes, you tend to act overly dominant and possessive.

You must rationalise events and be more realistic towards the faults of others. Be more receptive of others' viewpoints.

The D type

You are cynical, distrustful and impatient. You tend to lose control easily and may have a tendency towards violence and aggression. You must remember that to be a model parent, you must act in the same way as you would like your child to do in front of you.

SELF-IMPROVEMENT/PERSONALITY DEVELOPMENT

Also Available in Hindi   Also Available in Hindi   Also Available in Kannada, Tamil

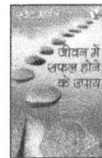      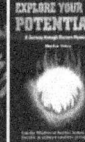 

Also Available in Kannada

Also Available in Kannada

All books available at www.vspublishers.com

RELIGION/SPIRITUALITY/ASTROLOGY/PALMISTRY/PALMISTRY/VASTU/HYPNOTISM

CAREER & BUSINESS MANAGEMENT

Also Available in Hindi, Kannada

Also Available in Hindi, Kannada

Also Available in Kannada

Contact us at sales@vspublishers.com

QUIZ BOOKS

ENGLISH IMPROVEMENT

ACTIVITIES BOOK

QUOTES/SAYINGS

BIOGRAPHIES

IELTS TECH

CHILDREN SCIENCE LIBRARY

Set Code: 02122 S

Set Code: 12138 S

COMPUTER BOOKS

Also available in Hindi   Also available in Hindi

All books available at www.vspublishers.com

STUDENT DEVELOPMENT/LEARNING

POPULAR SCIENCE

Also Available in Hindi

Also Available in Hindi   Also Available in Hindi

PUZZLES

Also Available in Hindi   Also Available in Hindi

DRAWING BOOKS

Also Available in Hindi   Also Available in Hindi, Tamil & Bangla

CHILDREN'S ENCYCLOPEDIA – THE WORLD OF KNOWLEDGE

Contact us at sales@vspublishers.com

www.ingramcontent.com/pod-product-compliance
Lightning Source LLC
Chambersburg PA
CBHW070517100426
42743CB00010B/1844

Praise for "Why Not Forgive"

"In the book *Why Not Forgive?*, Cassie Williams gives biblical-based and practical wisdom on why we should forgive. It's not just for ourselves but for generations that come after us. Forgiveness is what God gave us, and we are to forgive others."

~ **Thomas Hatten**, U.S. Navy, Ret

"Cassie opens up about the emotions and feelings she found herself navigating in her tender years. A sensible choice to choose love and forgiveness that surpasses understanding: not because we are without fault but despite the wounds of life.

Cassie addresses the issues one faces through life and battles of the mind that reason in the flesh. She takes the reader through the layers and stings of unforgiveness. The relevant nature of convening the raw truth of life and choices affects all who either make a choice or choose for others. *Why Not Forgive?* is a healing process, refreshing the soul and the compass to the way out!

As a reader, given the opportunity and steps to identify the lasting effects of trauma and life experience resulting in unforgiveness, the response to the situation impacts how one sees life. Cassie draws attention to humility's key to releasing the mind held captive by unforgiveness. Don't go it alone! Knowing our heavenly father equips us with forgiveness through God's love.

Why Not Forgive is a sobering reminder that one's destiny does not have to be what one may suffer at the beginning of life's emotional pain and hurtful relationships."

~ **Pastor Lily Rodriguez**, B.S., East End First Assembly of God Galveston, TX LA Women's District Director